THE ANIMATION BOOK

Peter Viska

SCHOLASTIC INC.
New York Toronto London Auckland Sydney

ISBN 0-590-47573-8

12 11 10 9 8 7 6 5 4 3 2 1   3 4 5 6 7 8/9

Printed in the U.S.A.   08

First Scholastic printing, October 1993

CONTENTS

INTRODUCTION

Animation is the process of bringing something to life—making it come alive and move. It's a lot of fun, but it's also a lot of hard work. The good news is that you don't have to be a genius or a great artist to do it. Seeing your characters move is one of the greatest creative thrills you can experience.

This book shows different types of animation, different ways of making things move, and some tips and advice on how to have fun and enjoy the thrill of animation.

Animation means much more than the cartoons you watch at home on the television. With the help of your imagination, some understanding of movement and, of course, this book, you can learn how to amaze your friends with your efforts. Dazzle them with your knowledge of animation terms. Design animation characters. Plan animated sequences. Show off with plasticine animation, face-mation, pixilation and, of course, cel animation. The instructions have been kept simple, but remember—practice makes perfect, so be patient!

Animation. It's good fun, and who knows?—in a few years time you could start your own

.... LAND.

(Print your last name on the dotted line.)

PAINT BRUSHES

WATER BASED PAINT

PAINTS ↗

PLASTICINE ↘

PLASTICINE

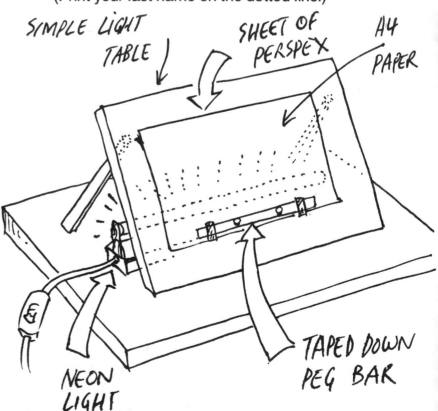

SIMPLE LIGHT TABLE ↓

SHEET OF PERSPEX ↙

A4 PAPER ↙

NEON LIGHT

TAPED DOWN PEG BAR

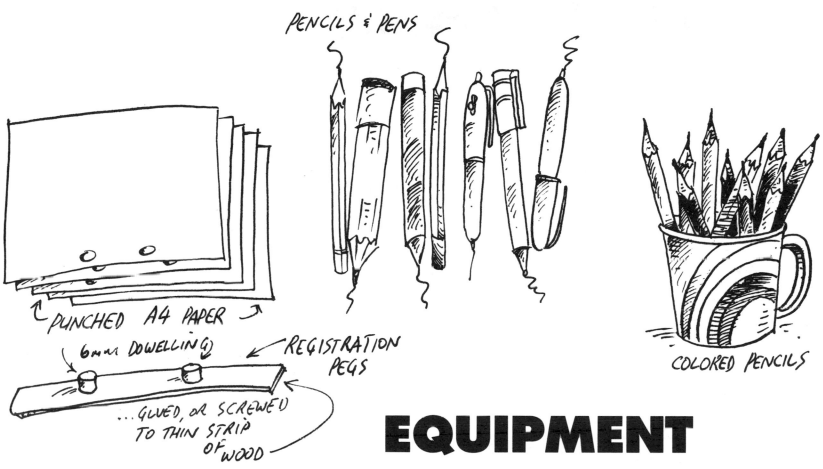

PENCILS & PENS

COLORED PENCILS

PUNCHED A4 PAPER

6mm DOWELLING

REGISTRATION PEGS

...GLUED, OR SCREWED TO THIN STRIP OF WOOD

COMMON 2-HOLE PUNCH

EQUIPMENT

As you can imagine, setting up your own studio can be very expensive, but for you to do your own animation, or to make your own short animated film, we have included a list of hints and inexpensive alternatives to expensive equipment.

You also need a video camera or a movie camera to film your animation. These can be borrowed, or hired from a camera shop.

Lights are also needed for model and plasticine animation. Use bedlamps and reading lamps.

A tape-recorder is handy to help with your sound effects.

ANIMATION TERMS

Before you become an animator it is important to talk like one. Here are a few vital terms and sayings that will make you sound very experienced. By the time you finish the book you may even know what they mean.

TERM	WHAT IT DOESN'T MEAN	IT MEANS
Layout	What you'd like to do when you've been drawing for ten hours straight.	Your plan—a series of drawings which show what action will take place in a scene.
Anthropomorphic character	A tropical ant farm.	An animal character that has human form or personality.
Key poses	People who hang around on the beach and show off their muscles (not mussels).	The main animation drawings.
Inbetweens	The ingredients of your sandwiches when you're hard at work, ie 'Please inbetween some bread with Vegemite, Dad, so I can keep drawing.'	The drawings that fill in the movement and join up the drawings of the key poses.
Walk cycle	What you have to do when your bike has a flat tire.	A certain number of drawings that are filmed over and over again in order, so that it seems that the character in them is walking.
Lip sync	A basin in which to wash bits of jam and doughnut off your mouth.	Making the mouths of the characters correspond to the words they are saying.
Cel	What they put you in when you start to believe that mice and rabbits can talk and that Marge Simpson is a real person.	A clear plastic sheet onto which the drawings are traced.
Zip pan	A pot in which to cook flies.	When the camera moves quickly across the drawing.
Pixilation	When you start to see little people with pointy ears running around on the page when you've been drawing for ten hours straight.	Stop-frame (frame by frame) filming of still objects, that appear to move when film or video is played.
Clean up	What you're asked to do when you've got carried away and left paper, pens and paint all over the house.	Making the final drawing look neat and tidy.

WHAT IS ANIMATION?

Animation is the process of bringing something to life. Animation happens when a series of pictures are shown one after the other to trick your eye into believing that they move. This is what happens when your eye and brain join up the carefully spaced pictures which are flashed on film or television.

The best way to see this happening is to play with a flip book. Even though each drawing can be quite different, when they are seen one after the other, you believe that the drawings move.

FILMING

SHOWING YOUR ANIMATION . . .

ON VIDEO ↗

ON FILM ↗

ON COMPUTER ↗

FLIP BOOK ↗

YOUR STORY

You can make up your animation as you go along, or you can plan it.

If you want to plan your animation, the best place to start is with a story.

Make up your story and either handwrite it, or type it on a typewriter or a computer.

Start your story with a quick story-line.

The story-line should give an overview of the action and the plot without giving too much detail.

For example, the story-line of *The Three Little Pigs* would read: three young pigs leave home, build houses of different materials, have separate conflicts with a wolf who has his end scalded, in the end, at the house of bricks.

As you get better with your stories you can try to convert them into scripts.

Your script needs a title.

Next, invent characters, with a brief description of each.

To make the characters interesting, think about different sizes, shapes, mannerisms and colors.

Once your story starts, you also need to set up a scene where the action is happening. Decide what time (day, night, dusk, etc) it happens, and then give some detail of what the people actually say.

Here is a sample of a script . . .

Characters

Sam
Happy, tall and a bit clumsy.

Sue
Detective type. Know-it-all.

Ben
Little brother. No front teeth.

Scene 1
Daytime. Inside cubbyhouse.
The two boys flash their torches
onto an old book.

Sam
'Look, a page is missing.'

Sue
'You're right. It's been ripped out.'

Ben (scared)
'What's that noise?'

The story needs to be done in a few stages or drafts.
In your first draft you can describe the time and
place . . . but once you have drawn or made your set
of the place, you don't need to describe it in words.
At this stage you concentrate on action or spoken
words.

CHARACTER DESIGNS

Before you can start any animation, you need a character or characters to play with in your story.

To design a character, start with a drawing—then play around with it to see what would happen if you made it bend down, call out, wave, run or walk.

Try to make your character original and different. Think of some special look or outfit.

Colors can also play a big part in character design.

Remember that you will have to make your character react or act, so you may need eyes, eyebrows, arms, head, body etc.

Try combinations of different head sizes to body sizes, different eye sizes, mouth sizes, teeth sizes, hairstyles and shapes. When you get better at animation it is possible to make even a brick act without eyes, mouth, arms or legs. After you design your characters, whether they be animals, people, monsters or crazy creations, draw them in different poses to show what they look like from the front, side, back, and a three-quarter front view.

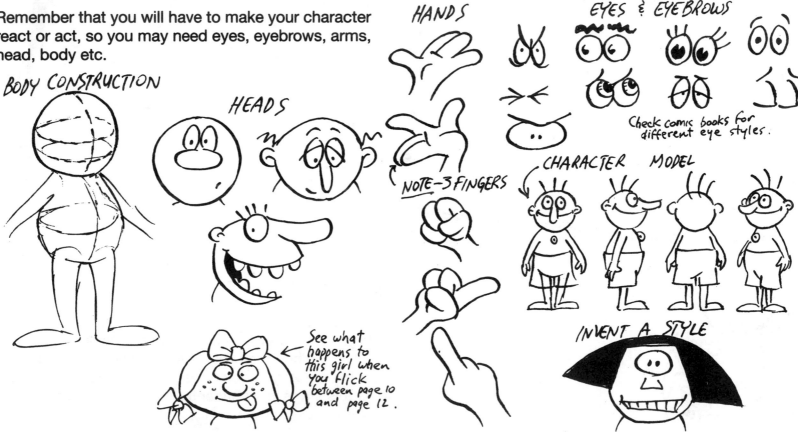

BODY CONSTRUCTION

HEADS

See what happens to this girl when you flick between page 10 and page 12.

HANDS

NOTE—3 FINGERS

EYES & EYEBROWS

Check comic books for different eye styles.

CHARACTER MODEL

INVENT A STYLE

10

ANIMALS

Ready? Now design some animal characters. You can use reference books to check on anatomy, but as long as your character looks like an elephant, it will be an elephant. Always keep your character design simple.

KEEP IT SIMPLE!!

INSECTS →

TOASTER

← OBJECTS →

PAINT BRUSH

PEOPLE

People characters are probably the easiest to design, but still try different sizes, shapes and outfits.

← Flip between pages 11 and 13 to see what happens.

11

Another great advantage of animation is the fun you can have with fantasy characters. You can design all sorts of monsters, crazy toasters, paintbrush people, smiling suns, bouncing water bombs and hopping aliens. With a little extra effort you can also create anthropomorphic characters of your own. Anthropomorphic is the term used to describe animal characters that act and perform as if they are humans.

CRAZY CREATURES

Anything goes when you design crazy creatures, but try to invent some funny actions to match their personalities.

MONSTERS

There is no limit to the ways you can design monsters, but remember, if your monster has a thousand eyes, you have to redraw those eyes every time it moves. Keep it simple.

ANTHROPOMORPHIC CHARACTERS

You can have extra fun with humanised animals by dressing them in normal or abnormal clothes or outfits.

KEEP IT SIMPLE.

STORYBOARDS

In animation and filmmaking, the storyboard is like a comic-strip version of the story or script. The storyboard allows you to visualise what the words say, so you can plan your animation drawings.

Storyboards are meant to be changed. Don't draw in too much detail until you are happy with the flow of the story.

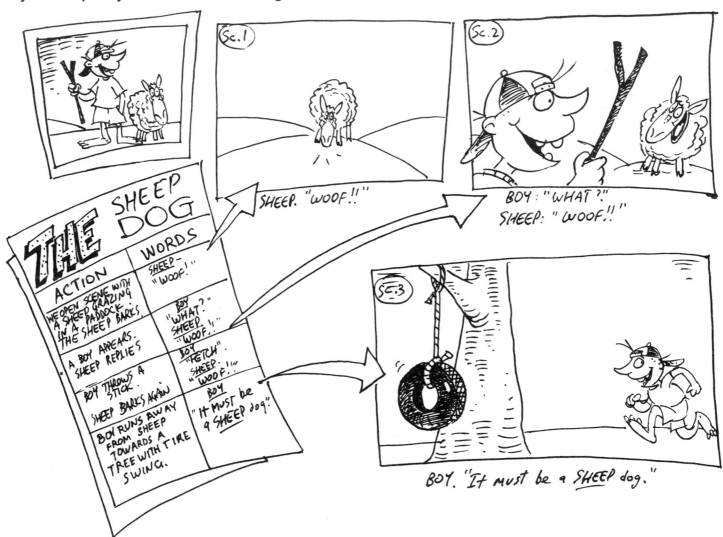

Sc.1

SHEEP. "WOOF!!"

Sc.2

BOY: "WHAT?"
SHEEP: "WOOF!!"

THE SHEEP DOG

ACTION	WORDS
WE OPEN SCENE WITH A SHEEP GRAZING IN A PADDOCK. THE SHEEP BARKS.	SHEEP – "WOOF!"
A BOY APPEARS. SHEEP REPLIES	BOY "WHAT?" SHEEP "WOOF!"
BOY THROWS A STICK. SHEEP BARKS AGAIN	BOY "FETCH". SHEEP "WOOF!"
BOY RUNS AWAY FROM SHEEP TOWARDS A TREE WITH TIRE SWING.	BOY "It MUST be a SHEEP dog"

Sc.3

BOY. "It must be a SHEEP dog."

Some animators make up a storyboard as separate drawings on cards. If you do this, it lets you pin them onto a pin board, and change one drawing, or their order, without messing up your main board.

TRY TO STORYBOARD A NURSERY RHYME.

THE ROO BOAT
OPEN ON TITLE

STORYBOARD ON A SINGLE SHEET OF PAPER.

PUSH PINS

ACTION

PIN BOARD

STORYBOARD DRAWINGS ON CARDS OR PIECES OF PAPER

SCENE NUMBER

Sc 14 ANDY— "Watch OUT!" ← DIALOGUE

YOUR STORYBOARD DRAWINGS CAN BE ABOUT THIS SIZE.

LAYOUTS

After a storyboard is completed, each scene is broken down into a background and its action levels. To plan the background, you design the layout (or stage where your character will appear) by redrawing and registering the background without the character that exists on your storyboard frame.

Make a photocopy or tracing of that background, and add to it your character as well as the starting and finishing poses of the action.

Sc.7

ELLIE – "Over here !!"

THE STARTING POINT — The storyboard frame

B/G ⑦

The layout for the background.

TRACE-OFF OF B/G LAYOUT PLUS ACTION POSITIONS.

PHOTOCOPY OF B/G LAYOUT PLUS ACTION POSITIONS.

Two different approaches to layouts.

Depending on how tricky your animation becomes, you can design backgrounds that are long, tall, or have amazing angles (perspective).

This long background layout allows the action to move across it.

Here is a layout for a waterfall background. The action has the boat approaching the edge.

This a down shot (view from above) with dramatic perspective.

This underground layout sets moods and dark tones.

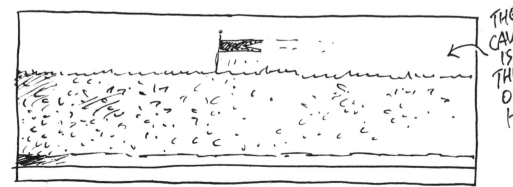

THE CAVALRY IS ON THIS SIDE OF THE HEDGE.

Background layouts like this let you have action happening behind a hedge, saving lots of animation work.

BACKGROUNDS

In animation, a background is a specially designed drawing of the scenery—your action takes place on it.

The background plus your animation drawing, is called a set-up.

By using the planning in your layouts you can make your stage as interesting as your imagination. Good backgrounds will make your animation look great.

A background, like any illustration, can be a drawing, a painting, a collage, a picture from a magazine, or just plain colored paper.

The background illustration can also be in colour or black-and-white, depending on your overall character designs.

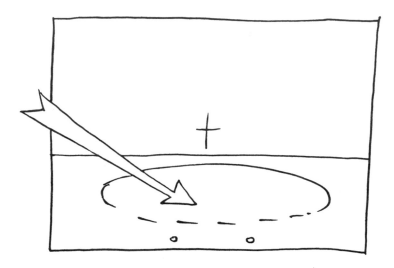

Here is an example of how the same acting space can be used in different backgrounds . . .

POND   ROOM   BACKYARD   MOON

Here is an example of a long background that has three positions on it. As well as your background, you can also add extra levels that go under the animation (called an underlay) or over the animation (called an overlay).

As your animation skills improve, you can learn how to use 'pans' with your long backgrounds. The character stays in one spot, while the background pans (or slides) beneath the animation. The result gives the illusion that the animated character is moving along the scenery.

You will start to notice the appearance of two circles at the bottom of animation illustrations. The circles represent a two-hole registration system that is explained in detail on page 32.

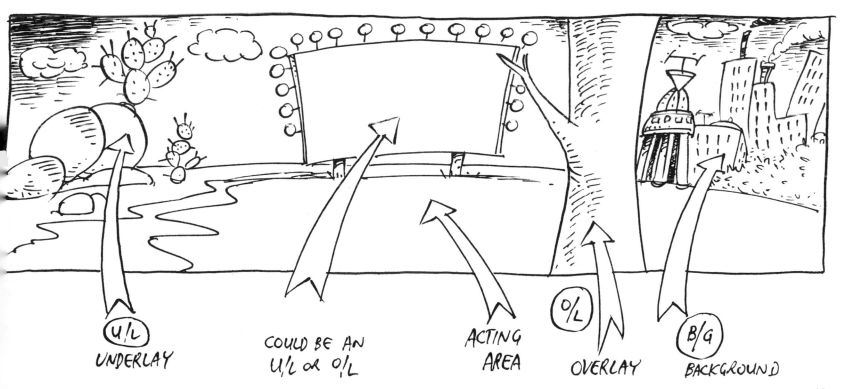

U/L
UNDERLAY

COULD BE AN
U/L or O/L

ACTING
AREA

O/L
OVERLAY

B/G
BACKGROUND

ANIMATION

HOW TO ANIMATE YOUR CHARACTER

Before you start animating, you need to guess how long to make your scenes and the action. This part of your planning is called timing. There is no exact answer to what is the right time. Whatever works is okay.

After you have designed your big or little characters, it is important to give them personality (or 'character'). As the creator, you decide what they do and how they do it. Whether your character is made of paper or plasticine, or is a drawing or a model, the only way to learn is to experiment.

It is easy to make an object or character move . . . but it is much harder to control the movement and the mood of your character. Practice makes perfect.

If you have a video recorder at home, you can study movement by watching the action frame by frame using the 'Pause', 'Play', 'Pause' buttons. You will see that little movement (especially in body, arms and head) = little action. The more action, the further apart the body, arms, legs, etc will be from frame to frame. Use this rule to control your animation to do the same thing.

How or where do you start to make your drawings appear to move? Your first step is to draw one of your characters in an interesting pose. Next, using your registration system (see equipment, page 4), draw the same character in another interesting pose that is related to the first drawing. After you have finished the second pose, draw the third pose, then the fourth pose, and so on until the end.

NOTE
To make life easier, use a light table (see equipment, page 4) to trace each pose from the pose drawing just before it. Flipping from one pose drawing to the other will show you if it appears to move.

Place (2) on top of (1) and flip from (2) to (1). It will appear to move. Then place (3) on (2) and (4) on (3).

After the rough animation drawings are completed on paper, they can be cleaned up, so that the character stays 'on model'. This means the character you draw always resembles your model sheet. A common problem is that with each drawing, the character starts to get a little bigger . . . so always check the size.

THE PROCESS FROM PENCILS TO CELS

Character as rough pencil drawing on paper . . .

as cleaned-up drawing on paper . . .

traced onto clear cel then painted on reverse side . . .

on cel on top of background.

ANIMATING TO A SYSTEM

Animation studios have developed a good system, where only the main pose drawings (called keys) are drawn first on paper. The animator guesses how many drawings are needed in between each key, and writes instructions on the key drawings. The next artist, called the inbetweener, draws the inbetweens that are needed to make the action flow when it is filmed. This is where the animator tells the inbetweener how many drawings are needed between each key. The more inbetweens, the slower the action. Whatever works is okay.

STRAIGHT-AHEAD ANIMATION

Another way of animating is to start with a good drawing of a character, then to make up your animation as you go. To do this, you need an idea of where you want your character and your story to go. Remember, keep it simple.

Metamorphosis is a fun version of straight-ahead animation, where you make your character change into a completely different character.

In this sequence the elephant has metamorphosed into a tennis racquet and ball. Metamorphosis (morphing) can also be done using plasticine animation, computer animation, flip books, and models.

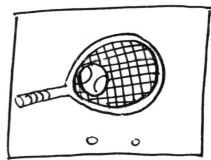

In order to make this metamorphosis (from elephant to tennis racquet) last two seconds, you need a total of twenty-five drawings from the first to the last picture. Then you will need to film every drawing for two frames.

Once you have started animating your drawings, you can have fun with a couple of classical animation exercises. Both will give you a taste of how you can totally control your characters' movements. The first is a bouncing ball and the second is called a walk cycle. Try both, then experiment with more or less action.

THE BOUNCING BALL

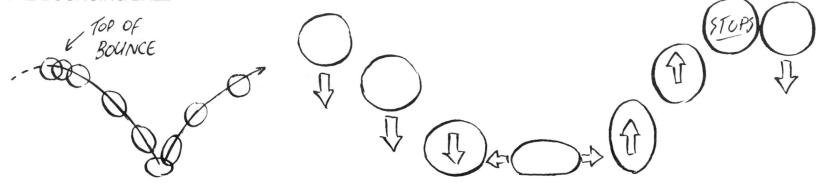

Animating the ball bouncing will introduce you to the effect of gravity. When the ball reaches the top of the bounce it almost stops before gravity pulls it down. As it starts to go down, it starts to accelerate until it hits the floor. Here it tries to continue, but the floor stops it. The ball squashes. The energy in the ball then overcomes gravity to push the ball up off the floor, where it slows to a stop again as gravity equals the force of the bounce. Down it goes again, and so on. By varying the drawings you can change the whole personality of the ball. A ping-pong ball will have a different personality from a tennis ball or a squash ball. Try to have your ball make itself bounce. First a movement, then a continuous bounce. After that you can change the same rules to make a frog bounce, or a diver bounce (ouch!). Make a round character of your own.

THE WALK CYCLE

A walk cycle is a series of drawings that animate the action of walking. If you analyze a real person walking on a treadmill or moving walkway, you will soon realize that the same action is used over and over. If the frame remains in the center of the screen and the background moves, this cycle can be drawn so that the drawing, like the steps, is repeated over and over. Most simple walk cycles have twelve drawings in the cycle where drawing number twelve is in fact drawing number one again. Here are some important points to remember in a walk cycle:

The position of the head is highest at drawings one and six because the legs are less bent at this stage. It is lowest at drawings three and nine.

Because your walk cycle has to lead back into drawing one it is important to include a little slip with each drawing to keep your character in the one spot.

Look carefully to see where feet and arms are at each stage of the step.

NOTE!
IT USUALLY TAKES ABOUT A SECOND TO WALK TWO STEPS. (ONE CYCLE)

NOW TRY A RUN

...AND A FAST RUN.

FLIP BOOKS

Although flip books are a primitive way of animating, they are still a good place to start in understanding many of the principles or rules of animation. Flip books need no special equipment and are very portable.

Most commercial flip books have about 40 pages of firm paper. You can make your flip book any number of pages you wish and, by experimenting with the paper, work out which flips best. The edges of notebooks are great to practice on, after you have finished your work. Make your flip book strong by stapling then taping the spine.

Hold the flip book in your left hand and flip the pages from front to back with your right thumb.

Try these flip book story ideas.

• The laughing face   • The jogger   • The falling cat

STAGES

1. Mess around with the corner of an old notebook to get the general idea of how a flip book works. Make up your story as you go along. Experiment.

2. After you have experimented, try to plan your story. Do this by making up a little storyboard.

3. Keep most of your drawing on the right half of your flip book.

To begin with, keep your story simple.

• The disappearing seal   • Tarzan swings   • The exploding clown.   • The steam train.

THAUMATROPE

A thaumatrope is a more scientific way of describing a simple spinning device that has part of a drawing on one side and the other part on the other side. When the device is spun, the drawings combine to make a complete picture.

Think of an interesting picture that can be made out of two drawings. Try a lady and her wig, or a hat and a bunny, a bird in a cage, or a bun and a burger.

Some thaumatrope ideas.

Front	Back

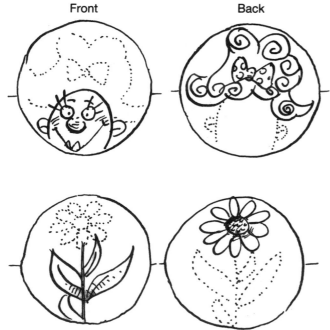

Front	Back

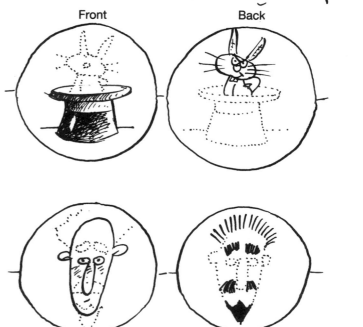

A thaumatrope can work horizontally or vertically, depending on which way it spins. Work out beforehand whether your drawing needs to be upside down or not as it spins.

How to make your own thaumatrope.

String

String

Start with a black-and-white illustration. If it works, add colour.

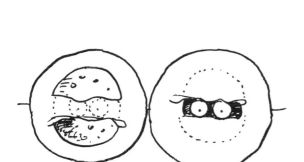

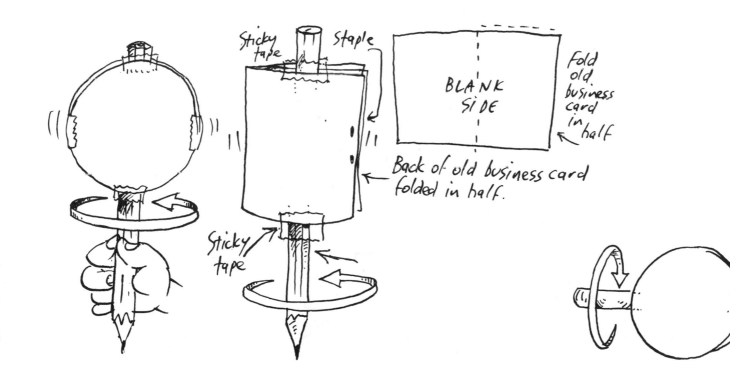

Sticky tape

Staple

BLANK SIDE

Fold old business card in half

Back of old business card folded in half.

Sticky tape

Pencil

ZOETROPE

A zoetrope is an optical toy in the form of a cylinder with a series of pictures on the inner surface which, when seen through slits when the cylinder rotates, give an impression of continuous motion.

Some zoetrope hints

1 Use a record player to rotate your zoetrope.

2 You need twelve images to make up your story.

3 The strips can be interchanged to make another story.

4 Make your strip story a twelve-drawing cycle so that it goes back to the start with each revolution.

A PERMANENT ZOETROPE HAS VIEWING SLITS BETWEEN ILLUSTRATIONS.

THE EYE SEES ONE DRAWING AT A TIME.

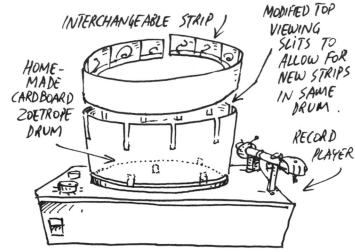

INTERCHANGEABLE STRIP

MODIFIED TOP VIEWING SLITS TO ALLOW FOR NEW STRIPS IN SAME DRUM.

HOME-MADE CARDBOARD ZOETROPE DRUM

RECORD PLAYER

Play at different speeds of 33 rpm or 45 rpm to see the difference.

You can make a zoetrope drum from firm cardboard, complete with slits, then make your own series of zoetrope strips that fit inside the drum. When the drum revolves, the view through the slits shows the pictures appearing to move. Like all animation, a certain amount of trial and error will improve your action.

Your zoetrope strip needs to have 12 frames, each measuring 4.8 cm x 5 cm.

REGISTRATION

As your line animation develops, you will soon realize that it is very important to make sure that artwork is kept still. Otherwise it wobbles when it is projected onto a screen. A system is also needed to make sure drawings that have been carefully designed to match or line-up, still do so when the camera films the animation set-ups.

These problems can be solved with a registration system. You can invent your own, or use a couple of these suggestions.

Most animation studios have a system using a bar which has pegs sticking up from it to allow paper, that has been carefully punched, to slide over them and sit firmly.

As it is difficult to obtain the use of an Acme standard hole punch, it is better to make your own system using a standard two-hole punch. You then need to make your own pegs to fit these dimensions. You may use wood, brass, plastic, iron or aluminium. Most animation is drawn with the registration holes at the bottom. This makes it easier to change drawings at the filming stage.

The two-holed registration system has been used for the animation in this book.

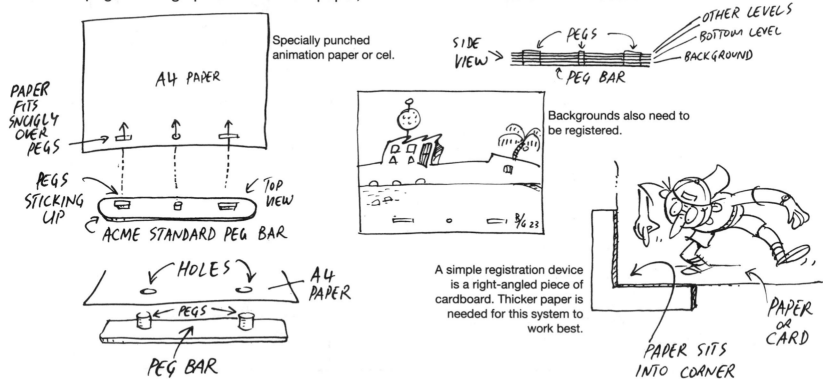

Specially punched animation paper or cel.

A4 PAPER

PAPER FITS SNUGLY OVER PEGS

PEGS STICKING UP

TOP VIEW

ACME STANDARD PEG BAR

HOLES — A4 PAPER

PEGS

PEG BAR

SIDE VIEW

PEGS

OTHER LEVELS
BOTTOM LEVEL
BACKGROUND

PEG BAR

Backgrounds also need to be registered.

A simple registration device is a right-angled piece of cardboard. Thicker paper is needed for this system to work best.

PAPER SITS INTO CORNER

PAPER or CARD

COLORING

Your approach to colors and the coloring of your animation will depend on which type of animation you use. Here are a few suggestions for the different drawn-animation techniques.

Try to invent your own way of coloring your work.

Paper

Drawing
+ colors
on
front

Funnel

CATSUP bottles

HOUSE PAINT WATER BASED

Paint

Glass jar with resealable lid

PAPER ANIMATION

First, draw your animated character's outline on each drawing, then go back and color each drawing. Experience will soon tell you to keep your colors to a minimum.

Choose, and keep to, a combination of colors for each character.

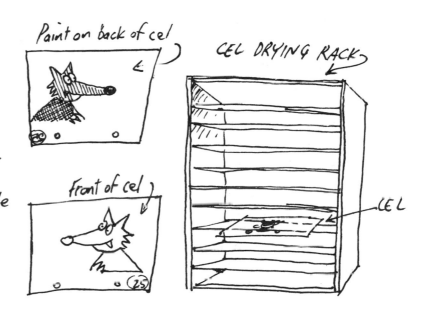

Paint on back of cel

Front of cel

25

CEL DRYING RACK

CEL

CEL ANIMATION

Here your character is drawn on one side of the cel, and on the reverse side, the character is painted with color.

The opaque color blocks out the background, the remaining clear cel allows the background to show through.

Hint: Keep the number of colors to a minimum. Special cel paints are expensive to buy, but an inexpensive alternative is the range of water-based acrylic house paints.

Different colors can be poured into clear plastic catsup squirting bottles for easy access. Old glass baby-food jars make excellent paint

containers. It is best to guess how much paint you will need for each character. That way, you can mix up enough in a batch to save you running out—otherwise you may have to try to mix and match the new color with the old.

In a studio, drying racks are used to keep the cels safe while they are drying.

SHOOTING YOUR FILM

After all your hard work, the time will come when you can shoot your animation onto film or video. Shooting your story will allow you to show all your hard work to your friends and your family.

METHODS OF SHOOTING YOUR FILM

HORIZONTAL
When filming in the horizontal position, it is most important that the camera is locked off. This means that the camera cannot be moved or shaken during filming. This can be done by putting strong masking tape or sandbags on the tripod feet.

VERTICAL
You need a stand to hold the camera steady while it points down to a table top. Set up the artwork with your registration system and film your work.

Animation can be filmed with a movie camera that shoots single frames of film, or it can be shot with a video camera. Most video cameras cannot shoot single frames, however, fun results can be achieved by the following method: press 'Record' on the camera for the shortest possible time, then 'Standby'. Modify your set-up, press 'Record' again for the shortest possible time, then 'Standby'. Change the set-up, press 'Record' then 'Standby'. Change the set-up, and so on for the length of the film.

Remember, work out a way to keep your camera very steady while you film.

The result you'll achieve using a video camera will be jerkier than the result using a movie camera, but

it is still fun to see, and you'll find the video camera much easier to obtain.

If your family, your school or a friend doesn't own a video camera, they can be hired from camera shops.

SOUND

TWO WAYS TO ADD SOUND TO YOUR PRODUCTION:

The next time you watch a cartoon on television, listen to how important the sound is to the overall picture. Sound is usually made up of the voices of the characters, and the sound effects.

IMAGE ON SCREEN

SPEAKER

AUDIENCE

1 Make all the sound effects as your animation is screened.

2 Pre-record your synchronised dialogue and sound effects onto an audio tape, then play it back while the animation is on the screen.

Ⓐ

MIKE

TAPE DECK

VIDEO TAPE PLAYER

Ⓑ

T.V.

START PICTURE AND TAPE AT THE SAME TIME.

BOING

OR

Ⓒ

DUB ONTO VIDEO PICTURE.

PIXILATION

Pixilation is the process of animation using stop-frame (frame-by-frame) filming with a camera that shoots selected frames of live action. Using this technique, you can produce some of the ideas on this page.

Plan storyboard.

The trick here is that only the frames you shoot will show. So, when they are joined up, you only see the plane flying in the air.

Cardboard plane and actor in flying clothes.

Choose position (A). Jump up at position (A), 'click'.

Move to next position (B).

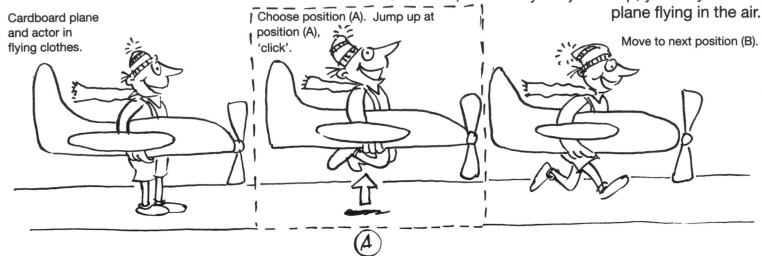

Ⓐ

You can also have fun without jumping.

Plan your storyboard first . . . and so on.

Caption B
Jump up at position (B), 'click'.

Move to next position (C).

Jump up at position (C), 'click'.

B

C

Here are some other ideas.

Note that by using only the frames you have shot (the ones marked 'click'), the end result will show a plane flying.

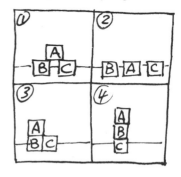

Try your own idea . . . a witch on a vacuum cleaner?

If you are shooting with a video camera, shoot on 'Record' for the shortest possible time, change the set-up, then shoot again for the shortest possible time.

FACE-MATION

Face-mation is a term used to describe the deliberate filming of someone's face to make a funny moving picture.

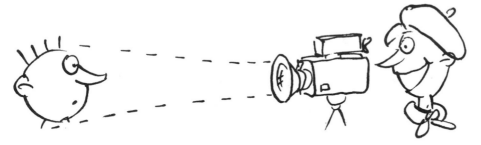

Ask a friend to stand in front of a video camera or film camera while you film a few seconds of a facial expression. Ask them to change their expression (eyes, eyebrows, mouth). Shoot a few more seconds of their face. Ask them to change expression again. Shoot another few seconds of their face.

There is not quite the need to storyboard this piece of animation fun. But it is advisable to plan ahead, so you can be prepared for the next pose or costume change, eg hats, masks, glasses or moustaches.

The same idea can be used with photographs or drawn faces on paper plates.

SOME IDEAS:

Film the faces of your friends, one after another. They can be dressed normally or dressed up.

Film each face for ten seconds.

Another method is to have them turn in front of the camera, revealing a new face for each turn.

FACE	TURN	BACK (PAUSE)	NEW FACE	CHANGE

DRAWING ON FILM

Before you start this type of animation, it is important to find a projector to show your work. Your school may have a 16 mm projector that your class is allowed to use.

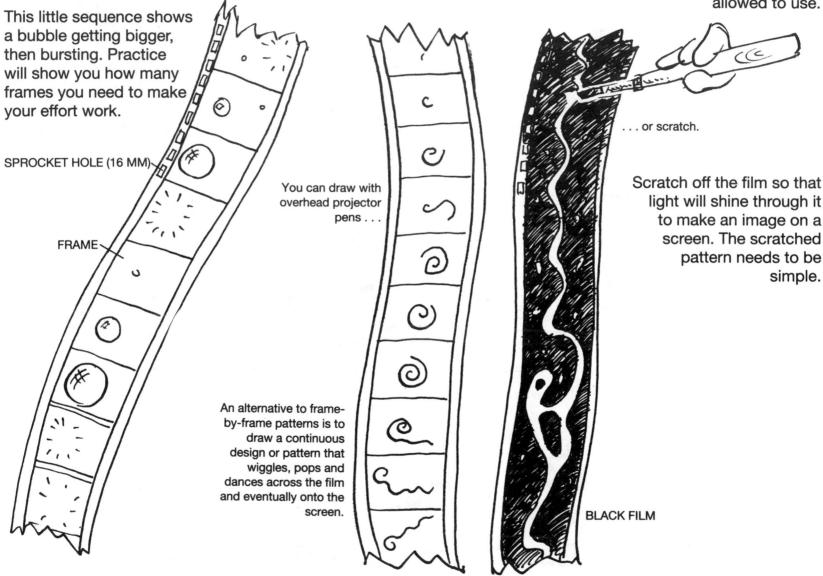

This little sequence shows a bubble getting bigger, then bursting. Practice will show you how many frames you need to make your effort work.

SPROCKET HOLE (16 MM)

FRAME

You can draw with overhead projector pens . . .

An alternative to frame-by-frame patterns is to draw a continuous design or pattern that wiggles, pops and dances across the film and eventually onto the screen.

. . . or scratch.

Scratch off the film so that light will shine through it to make an image on a screen. The scratched pattern needs to be simple.

BLACK FILM

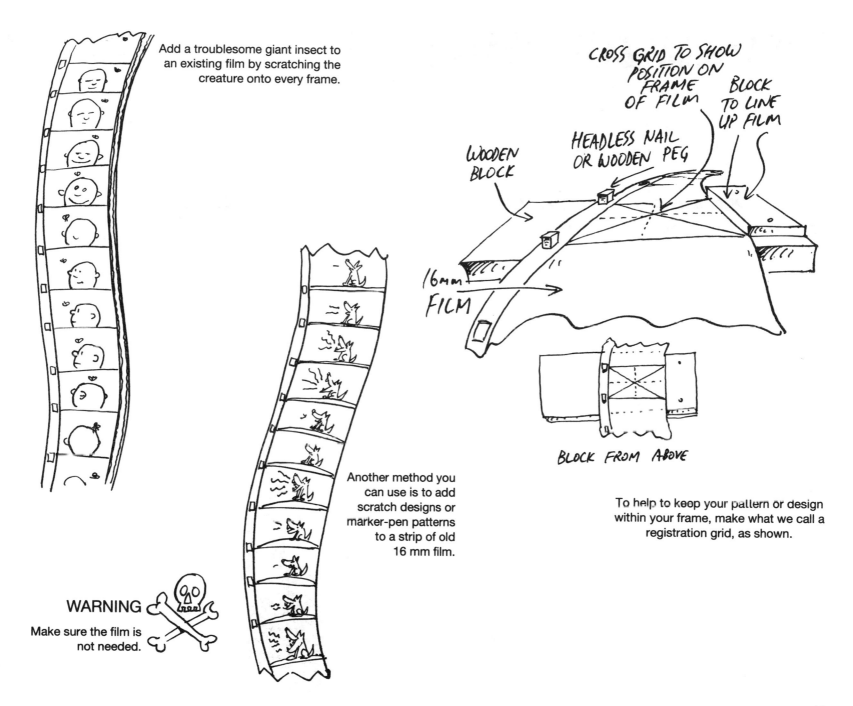

Add a troublesome giant insect to an existing film by scratching the creature onto every frame.

Another method you can use is to add scratch designs or marker-pen patterns to a strip of old 16 mm film.

CROSS GRID TO SHOW POSITION ON FRAME OF FILM

WOODEN BLOCK

HEADLESS NAIL OR WOODEN PEG

BLOCK TO LINE UP FILM

16mm FILM

BLOCK FROM ABOVE

To help to keep your pattern or design within your frame, make what we call a registration grid, as shown.

WARNING

Make sure the film is not needed.

41

PAPER ANIMATION

Paper is a wonderful medium to use in animation. You can draw on it, cut it out, use pictures printed on it, or you can make characters from it. Paper is also very inexpensive and its use is limited only by your imagination.

SOME PAPER ANIMATION TECHNIQUES

DRAWN CUT-OUT JOINTED CHARACTERS

Background.

Character.

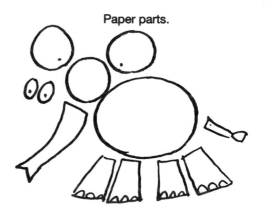

Paper parts.

PRINTED CUT-OUT

Old magazines can be a very helpful source of characters and extra bits. Try creating characters by using a head from one picture, arms from another picture, a dress from here and a mouth from there.

Paper animation is filmed in the same way as drawn animation, except instead of drawings you use your paper character or characters. There may be some problems with wobbling, but it is a fun method of animation. An easy-to-understand example would be a complex cut-out rocket ship flying across the background. Silhouette animation is another way to save hours of drawing.

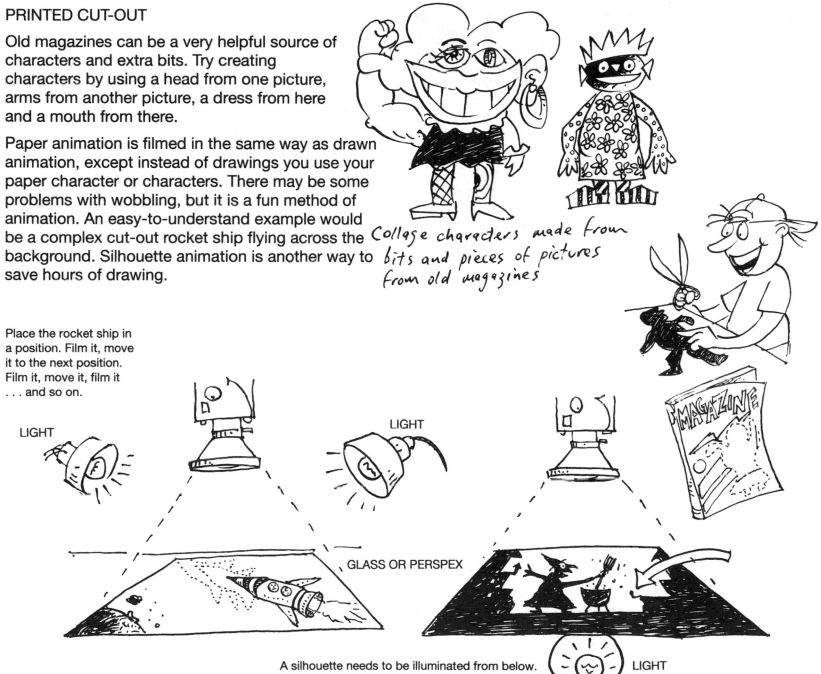

Collage characters made from bits and pieces of pictures from old magazines

Place the rocket ship in a position. Film it, move it to the next position. Film it, move it, film it . . . and so on.

LIGHT

LIGHT

GLASS OR PERSPEX

A silhouette needs to be illuminated from below. LIGHT

43

COLLAGE ANIMATION

YOU COULD MAKE UP A COLLAGE SET-UP LIKE THIS

FLAG FROM COLORED PAPERS

MATCHSTICK

A REAL PHOTO OF YOUR HEAD AND FACE

TEDDY CUT OUT FROM A TOY CATALOG

JAM JAR FROM A MAGAZINE AD.

HAND FROM BEAUTY AD.

BLUE AND GREEN CELLOPHANE PAPER FOR WATER

FRUIT FROM YOGURT AD.

THINLY CUT COLOURED STREAMERS

HAT ARTWORK FROM A FASHION MAGAZINE

HAND-KNITTED WOOLEN MINI SCARF

REAL COTTON MATERIAL FROM OLD SHIRT OR DRESS

SKY HAND-PAINTED ON PINK PAPER

Instead of drawing your animation, you can have fun with collages. To do this, cut out interesting characters from old magazines and then carefully cut off the arms, legs, heads, etc and work out a way to make them move. While you are filming you carefully move the cut-out characters, then film another set-up. A little piece of Blu-Tack helps to keep pieces of your character under control.

Warning: Do not sneeze!

With collage animation you can have maximum fun, without having to draw at all. You still need to plan what your cut-out character is going to do, and where.

Another way you can use collage animation is to start with a simple collage image, then, by adding little cut-out pieces, make a different image.

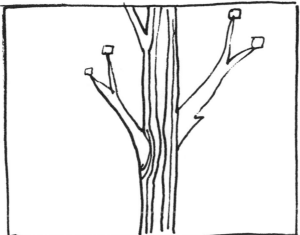

Simple collage starts with a tree trunk.

Frame by frame the tree grows faces.

Along comes a collage character without a head

. . . and chops the tree down.
A head falls on its shoulders and the character smiles.

45

PUPPET ANIMATION

Your puppets for animation can either be character puppets you already have, or you can make up your own. Like any character, the range is limitless, but personality is very important.

What you see on the screen.

The stage setting.

FILMING

Puppets are good subjects to animate but, as with models, you still need good planning.

46

When filming puppets, you need a story and a script. Keep the number of talking characters to a minimum. Rehearse your scene and, if necessary, use cue cards with the words you are going to act out printed on them. When you are acting and working your puppets at the same time, try to concentrate on opening and closing your puppets' mouths at the right times.

The end result.

Even TV productions use cue cards.

SCENE ONE

KOALA
YOIKS! THESE LEAVES ARE AWFUL.

ECHIDNA
WHAT DO YOU EXPECT?

KOALA
NOTHING —
NOTHING-BUT THE BEST!

Open hand.

47

MODEL ANIMATION

Model animation uses the same ideas and rules as drawn animation. The models are filmed frame by frame, move by move. They can be made out of plasticine, tin cans and magnets, blocks or little bottles, jars or boxes. Most recyclable objects can become characters.

STEP ONE: CHARACTERS

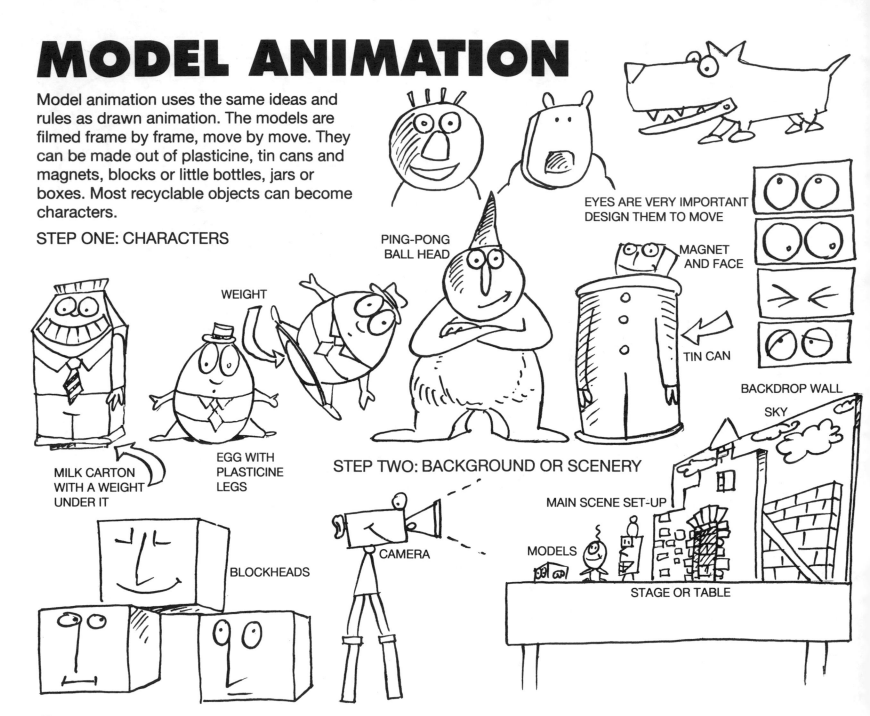

EYES ARE VERY IMPORTANT
DESIGN THEM TO MOVE

PING-PONG
BALL HEAD

MAGNET
AND FACE

WEIGHT

TIN CAN

BACKDROP WALL

SKY

MILK CARTON
WITH A WEIGHT
UNDER IT

EGG WITH
PLASTICINE
LEGS

STEP TWO: BACKGROUND OR SCENERY

MAIN SCENE SET-UP

MODELS

BLOCKHEADS

CAMERA

STAGE OR TABLE

48

STEP THREE:

PLAN THE STORY AND THE ACTION.

As in drawn animation, if you draw a storyboard it will help you work out your scenes and shots.

Use a storyboard to plan your scenes.

Rehearse your planned moves and check your timing.

If you have editing facilities you can use a clapperboard to keep track of scenes and takes.

TRIAL AND ERROR SYSTEM

By adding movable plasticine eyes and a mouth you can make your character act and react.

Only trial and error will show you how much to move your character and its parts.

STEP FOUR:

After you are happy with the look of the set-up and the lighting through the camera, shoot a few frames of your character, move the character slightly, shoot a few more frames, adjust your character, shoot, adjust, shoot, and so on. You will soon learn if your moves are too big (the action will be hard to follow) or too small (nothing much happens). Adjust your moves and keep practicing until you are happy with the effect.

MODEL-MAKING NOTES

To save a lot of time and money, use objects you find in or around your home for models and scenery.

It doesn't matter what it is made from, as long as it looks good through the camera.

Paint your scenery or characters with water-based house paints to add color or age.

Be careful not to get paint on your clothes.

MOTOR-DRIVE ANIMATION

This is a form of animation achieved by using a camera which has a special attachment that allows you to rapidly photograph action sequences.

Motor-drive animation can be an expensive but very interesting exercise.

First, borrow a motor-drive camera from a friend, or hire one from a camera shop.

1. Plan what action you wish to photograph.
2. Photograph the action with the motor-drive camera.
3. Develop the film.
4. Enlarge the photographs on a photocopier.

5 Arrange the photocopies in order, registering each one with the one before.
6 Color in the photocopies with pencil or opaque markers to liven up the image.
7 Film or video the pictures.
8 Try to cycle the pictures to get longer screen time.
9 Play the film back on screen or television.
10 Add a funny soundtrack.
11 Try a different motor-drive animation.

NOTE: If you can't borrow or hire a motor-drive camera, you could achieve the same effect by asking a friend to do something in slow-motion so you can photograph it with an ordinary camera, then just follow the instructions, starting with step 3.

SUGGESTIONS

Someone skipping.
Two people dancing in a circle.
A horse or dog running.
A friend doing cartwheels.

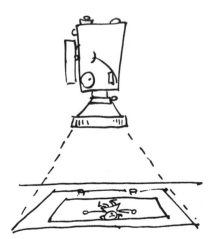

CEL ANIMATION

A cel is the term used for the clear acetate sheet used in animation. Originally it was made from cellulose, hence the word cel. The main advantage of using cels in your animation is that they are transparent. This means the camera can see the background through the cel and the background doesn't have to be redrawn or repainted each time. Cels can also save the animator a lot of extra drawing. This is especially so in what we call limited animation, in which only selected body parts move.

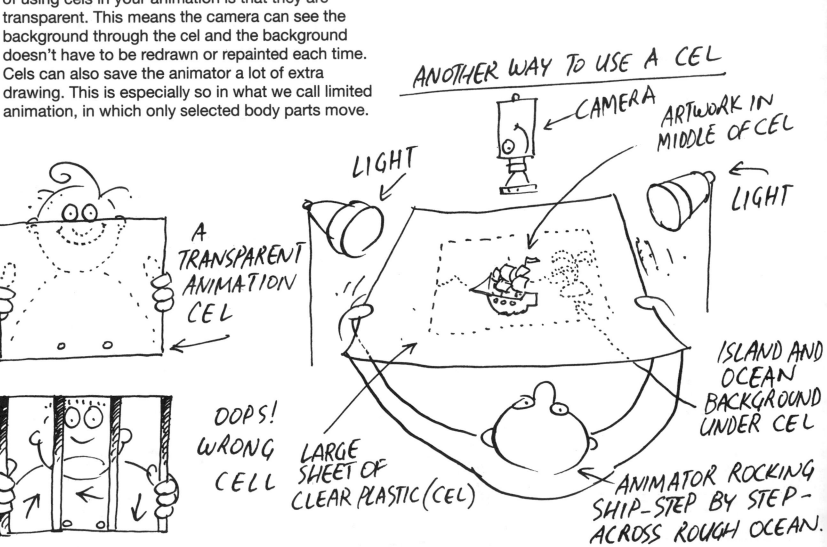

ANOTHER WAY TO USE A CEL

CAMERA

ARTWORK IN MIDDLE OF CEL

LIGHT

LIGHT

A TRANSPARENT ANIMATION CEL

ISLAND AND OCEAN BACKGROUND UNDER CEL

OOPS! WRONG CELL

LARGE SHEET OF CLEAR PLASTIC (CEL)

ANIMATOR ROCKING SHIP—STEP BY STEP— ACROSS ROUGH OCEAN.

HOW CELS WORK FOR YOU

THE SYSTEM

After you are happy with your line animation on paper, trace your character onto the cel—which is also punched and registered. (Try different pens or markers to see which give you the best image. Overhead projector pens are good to use.) Remember to number each cel. Also remember to place a little 't' for 'traced' on your paper drawing.

From your model-sheet, paint each character on the reverse side of the cel. This keeps your line drawing safe and neat.

NOTE: Cels can be purchased from an art or animation supply shop, but they are expensive. Look around to find other clear plastic you can use. Book-covering plastic is much cheaper, but you have to cut it yourself.

With limited animation where you want only some of the body to move, cels allow you to add different levels (for example arms) without completely redrawing the character. This system takes a little more brainpower, but it saves you heaps of time and drawing. This simple character is made up of different layers, as shown below.

Select a registered clear cel.

Place it over your paper.

Trace the paper image onto the cel.

When the segments on all levels are registered, they recreate the character. Remember, keep it simple! Too many levels are very difficult to handle and film.

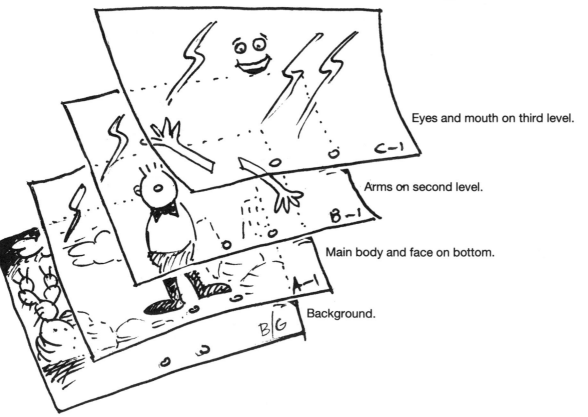

Eyes and mouth on third level.

C-1

Arms on second level.

B-1

Main body and face on bottom.

A-1

B/G

Background.

CELS CAN ALSO HELP PAPER ANIMATION

By cutting out and sticking your paper or line animation drawings onto a cel, you can use the same background without having to redraw it. This method also allows you to draw onto the paper with colored pencil before you glue it onto the cel.

Cels have to be numbered and registered.

COMPUTER ANIMATION

Every year sees exciting animation software packages for home computers. All computers are suitable for animation software, but some PCs give much better animation value for your money. New computer animation software packages are being invented regularly, so check out your local computer shop for the latest and greatest, or updates.

Most of the animation software available has its own approach to the animation process, but with a little practice you can see amazing results in a short time. It is necessary to be aware of animation terms mentioned earlier in this book, and the fundamentals of getting your image to move (see page 6 for terms).

THE PROCESS

As we mentioned in the earlier chapters, it is important to plan your animation before you start.

The same goes for computer animation.

Try not to be too ambitious with your first attempt. Computer animation uses a lot of memory, so you won't be able to animate more than about ten seconds at a time.

The programs on different systems vary slightly. Basically, though, you will need to:

1 Nominate (guess) how many frames you want to make your sequence.
2 Draw in each frame.
3 Press 'Animate'.

Most systems run the action in a cycle which lets you see the work over and over.

Of course, the process isn't quite as simple as that.

You can draw for the computer with the mouse, but that's like drawing with a brick. Depending on the system you use, you may have to save every frame in the memory and number it. In some systems, the computer will do this for you.

Then, step by step, after you have saved the image, you move onto the next frame. Carry forward the image you want to keep. Then cut and paste (for example) an existing arm in a new position. Save . . . and so on.

A special chart allows you to hold images for as many frames as you like.

MOUSE

MONITOR

ANIMATOR

MOUSE

FRAME 12/25

MOUSE PAD

KEYBOARD

The computer animation image can be drawn with the mouse or, with the help of a special scanner, you can digitise artwork into the computer's memory. The artwork can be your drawing or any drawing. It can even be a picture from a magazine or book.

Once the image is in the computer you can save it, then move it around, draw on top of it in the computer, or you can cut and paste sections of it.

You can make a mouth smile or talk, an eye close to blink, or an arm wave. If you digitise, you have to number the images in order, for example Dog 001, Dog 002, Dog 003, and so on.

Animation drawn on paper can be digitised, drawing after drawing, into the memory, and animated or cycled. Each drawing needs to be numbered in its order. After testing, line drawings can also be coloured by the computer.

Warning: Animation uses a lot of computer memory: Keep it simple!!

SCANNING CAMERA

DECODING BOX

CLICK

KEYBOARD

ARTWORK OR PAGE FROM A MAGAZINE BEING DIGITISED INTO THE COMPUTER

PRACTICE MAKES PERFECT

Quite often it is difficult to know where to start in the animation process. Here are a few exercises to make you practise a specific task. You can try these exercises with any type of animation listed earlier in this book. Try them as drawings or models.

1 THE WEIGHT-LIFTER

(a) Invent a character.

(b) Design something for the character to lift.

(c) Animate the character approaching the weight.

(d) Make the character lift or try to lift the weight.

(e) Invent a funny ending.

2 NUMBER CHANGES

(a) Invent a character in the shape of the number 1.

(b) Have the character do a funny action, then bend over.

(c) Make the character metamorphose (change) into the number 2 as it straightens up.

(d) Have the number 2 character make a funny action, then bend over.

(e) Make the number 2 character metamorphose into the number 3 as it straightens up, and so on for as many numbers as you wish.

3 A GREAT FALL

(a) Design a character called Humpty Dumpty and draw it onto a fresh egg. Use pencils, felt-tip pens, opaque markers, or paints to draw the face, body, clothes.

(b) Set up a stage that allows Humpty to climb onto a wall . . . steps? . . . a ramp? . . . a lift? . . . a crane?

(c) With the use of plasticine or Blu-Tack on the bottom of the egg, animate and film Humpty waddling along the wall, looking over, waddling left, then right, looking over, leaning back, leaning over . . . then toppling and smashing after his fall.

(d) Clean up the mess.

4 JACK BE QUICK

(a) Design an elephant character called Jack.

(b) Design a storyboard showing heavy Jack trying to jump over a candlestick. He succeeds, but his tail catches fire. He then puts out the fire.

(c) Plan a layout for this action.

(d) Roughly animate Jack and his adventure.

(e) How is the fire extinguished?

FUN WITH YOUR FRIENDS

The main problem with animation is that it takes a lot of work to produce relatively little on-screen time. To alleviate this situation, it is recommended that you try a group activity. With everyone adding a few seconds, you can easily animate one minute of fun.

1 Decide which method of animation you will all attempt.
2 Decide on a theme or story. It works best if everyone starts, then finishes at the same place. Try starting with a magician's hat. The idea is for everyone in the group to animate something appearing out of the hat. That character or object does something that is crazy, then disappears back into the hat. The only rule is, that the hat can't be changed.

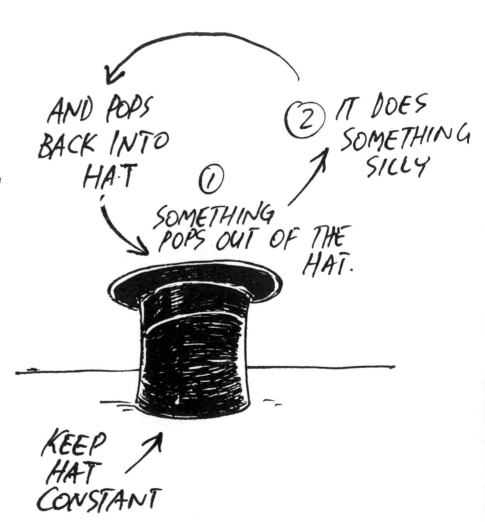

AND POPS BACK INTO HAT

② IT DOES SOMETHING SILLY

① SOMETHING POPS OUT OF THE HAT.

KEEP HAT CONSTANT

Other team ideas could be:

- Following a fly in its daily travels.

"YUM.. YUM!!"

- Start with the face of one member of the group, then each member of the group changes that face into their own.

- Start with a line across a page. Animate that line into the names of the members of the group, then back to the line.

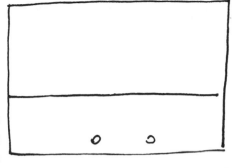

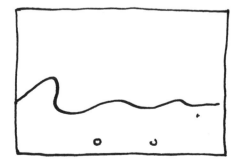

REFERENCES AND THANKS

REFERENCES

Here is a small list of very informative books on more advanced animation.

Each book has its own list of recommended reading, that also has its own list of recommended references—so good luck on your journey.

Blair, Preston. *Animation: Learn How to Draw Animated Cartoons.* Foster, 1949.

Gilliam, Terry. *Animations of Mortality.* Methuen, 1978.

Laybourne, Kit. *The Animation Book.* Crown, 1979.

Solomon, C and Stark, R. *The Complete Kodak Animation Book.* Eastman Kodak Company, 1983.

Thomas, F and Johnston, O. *Disney Animation: The Illusion of Life.* Abbeville Press, 1981.

White, Tony. *The Animators Workbook.* Watson-Guptill, 1986.

THANKS

A special thanks to the wonderful staff at Mickey Duck Animation Co, namely Lysette Ashford, David Cook, Bix Nussey and Andi Spark, for their invaluable help in getting this book to the publisher.

Thanks also to Greg Ingram and David Atkinson and to Helen Bateman for her patience and cool.